# OWLS

*created by*
## BOBBIE KALMAN

*art by*
## GLEN LOATES

BOBBIE KALMAN / GLEN LOATES

# OWLS

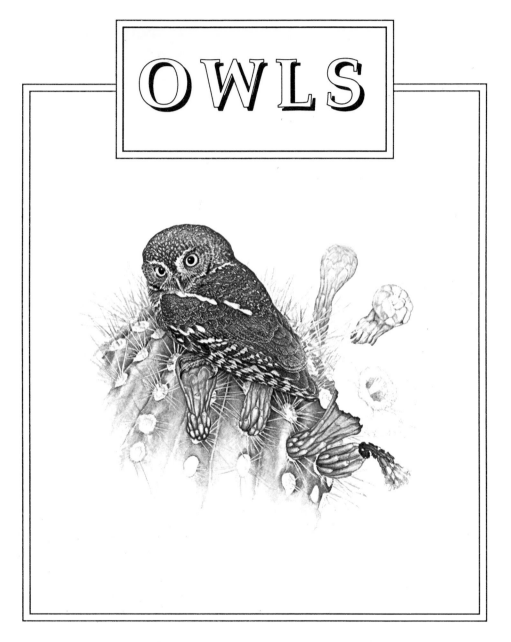

*The North American Wildlife Series*

**CRABTREE PUBLISHING COMPANY**

**The Glen Loates North American Wildlife Series:**
Created by Bobbie Kalman
Art by Glen Loates

**Editor-in-Chief:**
Bobbie Kalman

**Researcher:**
Anne Champagne

**Consultant:**
Kay McKeever

**Writing team:**
Bobbie Kalman          Christine Arthurs
Anne Champagne         Moira Daly
Janine Schaub

**Editors:**
Janine Schaub          Louise Petrinec
Moira Daly             Christine Arthurs
Anne Champagne         Judith Ellis

**Illustrations:**
Copyright © 1987 MGL Fine Art Limited.

**Photographs:**
Pages 14, 53: Barry Ranford/Used with the permission
of The Young Naturalist Foundation
Page 52: Bobbie Kalman

**Cover design:**
Leslie Smart & Associates Limited

**Page design:**
Stephen Latimer

**Computer layout:**
Christine Arthurs

**Mechanicals:**
Halina Below-Spada
Gerry Lagendyk

**Printer:**
Bryant Press, with special thanks to Arnie Krause

## For Kay McKeever

Cataloguing in Publication Data

Kalman, Bobbie, 1947-
        Owls

(The Glen Loates North American wildlife series)
Includes index.
ISBN 0-86505-164-X (bound)  ISBN 0-86505-184-4
(pbk.)

1. Owls - Juvenile literature.  2. Birds - North
America - Juvenile literature.   I. Loates, Glen.
II. Title.   III. Series: Kalman, Bobbie, 1947-
The Glen Loates North American wildlife series.

QL696.S8K34 1987   j598'.97'097

350 Fifth Avenue        120 Carlton Street
Suite 3308              Suite 309
New York                Toronto, Ontario
N.Y. 10118              Canada M5A 4K2

# Contents

# Who am I?

**L**ook into my eyes! Do I look magical or wise? Do I frighten you? I'm just an owl—neither wise, nor magical—but I'm sure you've heard the rumors about me by now. They have been around for thousands of years. People used to think that I could tell the future and predict births and deaths. What a hoot!

What am I really like? You might be surprised to find out that I am just one of 134 kinds of owls in the world. Each of us has individual looks and habits. You will meet my eighteen North American relatives right in this book. You can learn more about me too. Part of my name means "big." I am the second biggest owl in this book. Can you guess who-o-o I am? Be a wise owl and read on!

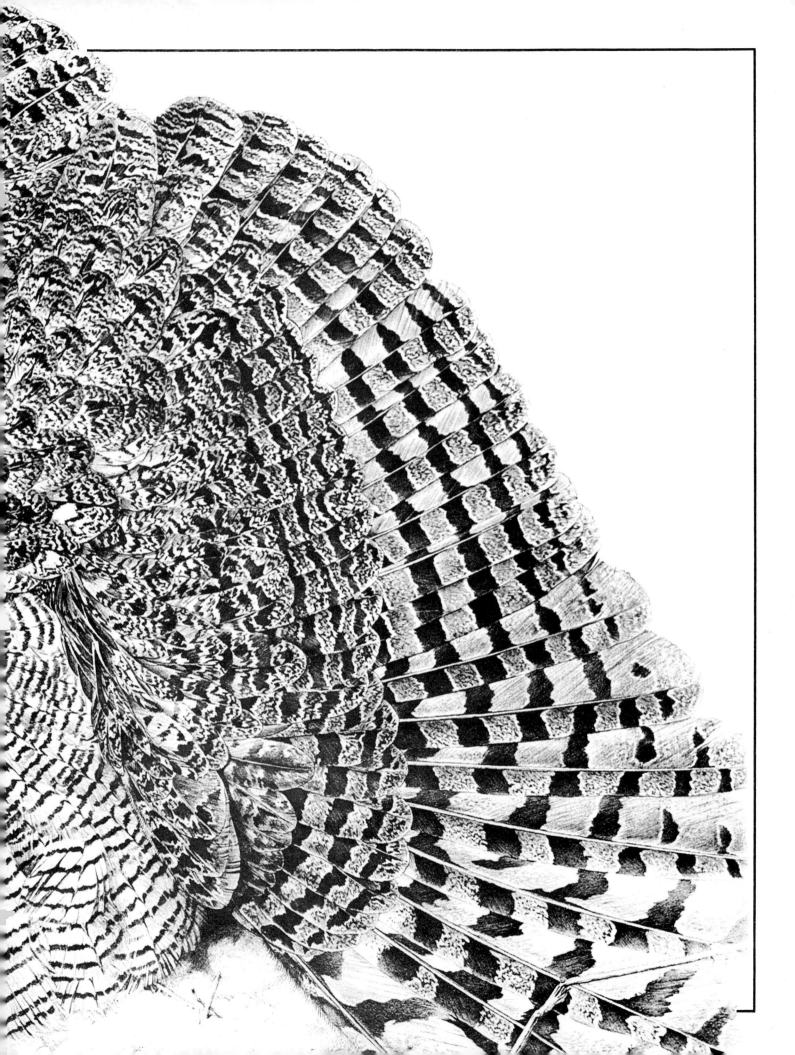

# The truth about owls

*A saw-whet owl*

Eagles, hawks, and falcons eat the same creatures as owls do. They hunt their prey during the daytime. Many owls hunt at night so there will be less competition for the same food. Nocturnal owls have special vision and hearing, which makes them excellent hunters.

## Are owls frightening?

Owls are known as **predators** and **birds of prey** because they eat other birds, insects, fish, and mammals. They have sharp **talons**, or claws, for catching their prey and hooked beaks for killing it and ripping it to pieces. These powerful killing tools have made some people fear these magnificent birds. For this reason many owls are shot each year.

*An owl talon*

Owls prey on living things in order to survive. They are not nasty or horrible because of what they eat. They are no more frightening than robins, which also eat living things—worms. People who eat meat could also be called predators.

## Where do owls live?

Most people think that all owls live in the forests of the north. Owls, in fact, live everywhere in the world except in Antarctica and on some islands far out in the ocean. Many do prefer living in the woods, but some make their homes in grasslands, deserts, and on the tundra of the far north. Several types of owls live high up in trees, some live on the ground, and a few make their homes in prickly cactus plants. One owl even lives in underground burrows.

## Are all owls nocturnal?

Although many people call owls **nocturnal**, which means "active at night," this label does not fit every owl. About half of all owls prefer dawn and dusk as their feeding times. There are even a few owls that hunt in the middle of the day! Owls that hunt during the day or at twilight are called **diurnal** owls.

## Who is hooting?

Most people think that all owls say "Hoo, hoo, hoo!" This is not so. You can hear the differences in owl calls if you train yourself to listen carefully. The calls can vary in the length of the song, the number of sounds, and the loudness and order of the sounds. Some owl calls even resemble the noises people make when they are laughing, crying, and snoring.

# Similar, yet different

**A**lthough owls have a similar appearance, there are many differences in their looks. Most owls have heads that seem large compared to the rest of their bodies and big eyes that resemble those of human beings. Their sizes, colors, and shapes, however, can be quite different. There are owls with large ear tufts and others with flat heads. Some have whiskers like cats; others have monkey-like faces.

## From huge to tiny

One of the most surprising facts about owls is the difference in their sizes. Some owls, such as the great gray and snowy, are huge. When the great gray's legs are fully stretched out, the owl can be as much as 75 centimeters tall from the top of its head to the tips of its toes. Most owls, such as the elf owl on this page, however, are a lot smaller than you might expect.

## Record and compare

Look through this book and record the name and size of each owl. Most of the owls are perching on branches. Their perching heights are given in each case. This is the measurement taken from the tops of the owls' heads to the bottoms of their feet. In pictures where an owl is shown standing or flying, the full height of the bird is also given. Make a graph showing the perching heights of the different owls. You may want to draw silhouettes or sketches of each bird to compare their different shapes.

*An elf owl shown actual size*

## Try this on for size

The tiny elf owl on the opposite page is exactly the same size as it would be in real life. The great gray and the barred owl on this page are not drawn to their actual sizes. They were drawn smaller so that they would fit on the page. If they are three times as large in real life, how many centimeters would they measure?

*A great gray owl*

*A barred owl*

# What do owls have in common?

## Facial disks

An owl's eyesight is twice as good as ours is in daylight, but what makes this bird truly special is its hearing. An owl rarely misses the smallest of noises. No one can ever sneak up and catch it by surprise!

On the faces of owls there are saucer-shaped hollows, called **disks**. Although these feathered disks are around the owl's eyes, they help the owl hear. When an owl is listening, it turns its face towards the sound. The sound waves are filtered through the hairlike disk feathers around the eyes and directed to the densely packed feathers along the outer edges. These feathers stop the sound and direct it further into the ear openings at the sides of the owl's head. It is believed that facial disks may make sounds louder!

## Tufts or no tufts?

Many people think that the feathers, or **tufts**, that poke up from an owl's head are ears. These tufts are not ears at all. In fact, they have nothing to do with hearing. An owl's real ears are hidden by feathers on the sides of its head. Owls use tufts to make themselves known to other owls in poor light. If one owl sees the outline of another perching owl at night, it is quickly able to tell what the other owl's message is.

*An owl's ears are hidden at the sides of its head.*

*A great horned owl*

## What do I mean?

If an owl's ear tufts are sticking straight up and forward, it means, "This is my territory and you'd better get out!" If the tufts are up and to the outside, it means, "I am not prepared to make any deals." If the tufts are down and back, it means, "Be gentle with me." Look at the owl on this page. What might its message be?

## Rubber necks

When an owl wants to look directly at an object, it has to bob, twist, and turn its head. Unlike human beings, whose eyes move in their sockets, an owl cannot move its eyes. To make up for having to stare straight ahead, an owl has an extremely flexible neck. Your neck only allows you to turn your head from shoulder to shoulder, but an owl can swing its head almost in a full circle. Its body can be facing forward, while its eyes are looking backward!

An owl has fourteen neckbones, while people have only seven. These extra bones allow the owl to move its head in almost any direction. An owl can move its head so easily that its neck appears to be made of rubber.

## Special eyes

If you came face to face with an owl, you would find yourself staring into huge, round, yellow or brown eyes. All the owls in this book have yellow eyes except for the barn, barred, spotted, and flammulated owls. Their eyes are dark brown.

The large eyes and pupils of owls are specially designed to let in extra light for seeing at night. In the back part of your eyes, and those of owls, are two kinds of cells that treat light in different ways. The **rod** cells gather light and help us see in poor light. The **cone** cells give us vision in bright light and enable us to recognize colors.

Nocturnal owls have many rod cells and few cone cells. As a result, they are colorblind, but they can see much better than we can at night! Diurnal owls, on the other hand, have more cone cells to match their daytime activity. No one knows for sure, but these owls may be able to see in color.

## Binocular vision

Whenever we look at something, each of our eyes sees a slightly different view of the same object, but parts of these views overlap. (Close one eye at a time to see how this works.) This overlapping view is called **binocular vision**. Owls have this same ability because their eyes are also in the middle of their faces. Binocular vision allows owls to judge sizes and distances accurately so they can swoop down and pounce on their prey. Other birds have eyes on the sides of their heads and have very little overlapping vision.

## Windshield-wiper eyelids

Owls and other birds have a third eyelid that humans do not have. This clear eyelid, called a **nictitating membrane**, moves across the eye sideways in the same way a windshield wiper does. It helps keep the eye moist and protected from dirt, especially when the owl is flying.

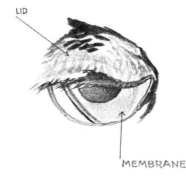

*The nictitating membrane*

# Food for owls

*Time for dinner!*

**M**ost owls eat only animal prey. Small owls gobble up insects such as grasshoppers, caterpillars, and beetles. They might also eat frogs, mice, and small birds. Big owls eat larger prey as well, such as lemmings, rats, squirrels, gophers, rabbits, skunks, and big birds.

Owls do not swallow their prey live. When they catch an animal such as a mouse, they quickly bite it at the back of its neck. The bite kills the mouse instantly, so it feels very little pain.

## One big gulp

Owls swallow most of their food whole. Even a three-week-old snowy owl can gulp down an entire mouse without chewing it at all! Swallowing the mouse is easy, but digesting it is a bit more of a task. You must be wondering what happens to the fur, bones, and claws when they arrive in the owl's stomach. You'd think they would give the poor bird indigestion!

Luckily, owls have very strong stomach juices that aid in the digestion of food. These juices help break down the prey while the owl's stomach muscles work to separate the tissues and animal parts that cannot be digested. These indigestible materials are then gathered into a neat package called a **pellet**. A pellet is made up of bones, claws, and teeth, all neatly wrapped in soft fur or feathers.

About five to eight hours after a meal the owl expels the pellet from its stomach. The fur or feather wrapping and a slippery coating from the owl's stomach make the pellet's passage along the owl's throat smooth and easy. An owl usually **regurgitates**, or spits up, one or two pellets every twenty-four hours, depending on the amount of food it has eaten.

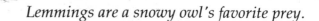

*Lemmings are a snowy owl's favorite prey.*

## Take a pellet apart

If you find a pellet, you can see for yourself what the owl ate. Soak it in warm water and then take it apart with tweezers. Lay out the bones, claws, teeth, fur, and feathers on paper. Now find a book about animal anatomy. Look at the different parts of the pellet with a magnifying glass and use the book to help you identify the bones and fur or feathers.

*An owl pellet*

You don't have to be worried about handling the pellet. Pellets are usually dry and clean. If you are still nervous about handling one, contact a company that supplies owl pellets to schools. These pellets have been further cleaned and treated.

## Food for my mate

Food is very important at mating time. In the spring a male owl hoots to attract a mate. He is announcing that he is in his territory. If a female appears, he often offers her a furry mouse to show her that he is a good hunter. After the couple have chicks, the parents must sometimes make twenty or more trips each night to catch food for their brood. In one summer a single pair of barn owls has been known to kill as many as 1500 mice!

If there is so little food around that chicks are in danger of starving, the bigger owlets often eat the smallest chicks in the nest. This way, a few strong birds are launched into the world. Owls need to be strong to survive the winter. It might seem cruel to eat the weaker young, but all the owlets in the nest might otherwise die.

*A saw-whet landing*

# Owl feathers

**H**ave you ever been surprised by an owl in the forest? Nocturnal owls can easily sneak up on people and animals because they are specialists at flying silently. An owl is so quiet that it can glide right by your ear and you may not hear it! Other birds make a whirring or whooshing sound as they fly. This sound is produced as the air rushes over the outstretched wings of the birds.

## Velvety feathers

An owl flies the same way as other birds do, but the feathers on its wings are covered with a velvety coating. This soft coating cushions the air as it rushes through the wings. It helps break up and scatter the sound. In addition, the feathers on the leading edge of the owl's wings have a fringe that resembles the teeth of a comb. Some people believe that this fringe helps cut down further sounds.

Nocturnal owls must be able to fly silently for hunting. If they had loud, flapping wings, they would not be able to hear anything but their own noisy flying! They would be unable to use their sensitive hearing to locate their prey. Diurnal owls that rely on their sight to locate food do not have these highly developed wing feathers.

_An owl feather_

_Notice the difference between the leading edges of these two feathers. The owl's feather has a fringe._

_A pheasant feather_

## Fluffing and flattening

Owls have a great deal of control over their soft, beautiful plumage. They can fluff up their feathers until they stick straight out or flatten them right against their bodies. Fluffy feathers are sometimes used to scare away intruders. If an owl is approached by an intruder, it puffs up to twice its normal size, spreads its large wings out, and sways from side to side. Its enlarged body makes it look mean and fierce.

_A great gray owlet covered in down_

## A protective coating

Owls have beautiful feathers that protect them from the wind and help keep them dry. Their feathery coats are usually gray or brown in color and patterned with streaks, bars, and spots. The design of an owl's feathers makes the owl resemble the background against which it is sitting. The color and pattern may look like plants in a meadow, the bark on a tree, or the snowy tundra. When a bird or animal blends in with its environment, it is hidden, or **camouflaged**. Owls rely on camouflage to protect them from their predators and hide them from their prey.

## Feather changes

When owls hatch, they are covered in a delicate layer of feathers called **down**. All young owlets shed a coat of down before their adult feathers come in. Northern owls keep their layer of cosy down under their outer feathers to protect them from freezing temperatures. Having this downy layer is like wearing long underwear. The shedding of feathers, called **molting,** continues throughout an owl's life as old feathers are replaced by brand-new ones.

# Barn owl

**H**ow would you feel if you met a pale-colored, knock-kneed, monkey-faced, dark-eyed creature in a graveyard? If you didn't know it was an owl, you might be afraid. It's no wonder that people in the past developed superstitions about this owl with spooky habits.

Many years ago people believed that the barn owl had supernatural powers. One of the reasons for this owl's ghostly reputation is that it was often seen in cemeteries. Its pale color, huge white face, and loud screeches would certainly have made anyone shiver!

If you were to spend time around a barn owl, however, you would soon find out that it is not such a scary creature. After all, its knock-kneed legs and heart-shaped face make it look more cute than frightening. Some of its calls might even make you laugh. Have you ever heard an owl hiss or snore? This owl does! Sometimes it says, "Get, get!" when it takes off.

*Barn owls like living on farms where there are plenty of mice. Farmers welcome these owls because they eat the mice that harm the crops. The hungry owlets in this barn nest are eagerly waiting for their parents to bring more food.*

## Scaring up supper

Barn owls are nocturnal. They search for prey where wildflowers and trees grow freely. To scare up a supper of sparrows, barn owls sometimes shake bushes with their wings. They have also been known to swoop down with a screech, making a mouse so frightened that it cannot move. At other times they grab their prey without a sound and swallow it whole. They can even dive into shallow water for fish!

18

*Barn owls are about 38 centimeters tall when they perch. The barn owl on this page would measure more because its legs are stretched out.*

# Long-eared owl

**A**lthough this owl is called "long-eared," it really doesn't have long ears at all! The tufts on top of its head are simply fluffy feathers. As explained earlier in the book, these tufts are for identification and not for hearing. The tufts of the long-eared owl look like vertical eyebrows, giving this owl a very wise and serious appearance.

## Full of tricks

At about 25 centimeters, the long-eared owl is a medium-sized owl. It is very good at defending itself against predators. One of its tricks is to make itself seem much larger than it really is. If an enemy comes too close to its nest, the owl hunches its shoulders and stretches its wings out like a huge fan. Sometimes it hops along the ground pretending to have a broken wing. This tactic steers intruders away from its precious eggs. The predator thinks the owl is wounded, so it follows the owl, hoping for an easy kill. Then the owl quickly flies away.

During the day the long-eared owl relies on its color and pattern to help camouflage itself against the bark of the tree on which it is perching. It stretches up tall and pulls its feathers tightly against its body. The striped, cream-colored feathers along its chest are marked with black and white. At night the long-eared owl flies from its roost to do its hunting.

## Owl or pussy cat?

If you hear a "meow" in the woods, it might not be a cat making the sound. It could be the cry of a long-eared owl! As well as catlike sounds, these owls make screeches, whines, and whistles as they fly through the forest.

# Short-eared owl

Can you guess where the short-eared owl got its name? You are right! It is named after its tiny ear tufts—so tiny, you can hardly see them! A short-eared owl is about 30 centi-meters tall. Its wings, though, are longer than those of other owls the same size. Longer wings show that this owl spends a lot of time flying.

From a distance, you might be able to spot a short-eared owl by the way it flies. It hovers in the air, seeming almost to float or drift, as a hawk does. Usually a quiet bird, this owl lets out a "Toot-toot-toot," or a "Boo-boo-boo," if you get too close to its nesting ground.

Short-eared owls are yellowish white with streaks of brown along their backs and on their pale bellies. They also have a circle of black feathers around their yellow eyes, making them look as if they have been in a fight!

## Open nesters

Short-eared owls prefer open places instead of woodlands and like to nest on the ground instead of in trees. Nesting on the ground can be dangerous, but somehow these owls manage to survive. They hide behind patches of wildflowers or grass, or they nest beneath shrubs in a meadow or marsh. While most owls are active at night, short-eared owls often hunt during the day, usually at dusk.

*The short-eared owl is related to the long-eared owl, although their habits are quite different. The long-eared owl is nocturnal and prefers living in forests; the short-eared owl is diurnal and lives in open places.*

# Great gray owl

The great gray owl is considered to be the largest owl in North America because it is taller from head to toe than any of the other owls. This tuftless gray bird can reach up to 60 centimeters when perching and 75 centimeters in full height. When it spreads its wings, the distance between the tip of one wing and the other is more than the height of an average eight-year-old child!

## Blending into the woodwork

If you wanted to see a great gray owl, you might have a difficult time. This owl avoids people, and its misty-gray coloring makes it difficult to spot among the gray, northern trees.

Great gray owls have more feathers than some other owls do because they live in northern areas. Layers of down and other feathers make these owls look larger and heavier than they really are. Great grays have almost ten centimeters of fluffy feathers on the tops of their heads!

## Where is that vole?

During the long hours of summer sunshine in the north the great gray owl hunts in the daylight. Its favorite prey is a mouselike rodent, called a vole, but it also eat birds, mice, frogs, and fish when voles are not available.

## All in the family

The great gray owl lays two to five small oval eggs every spring. The hatched owlets remain in the nest for about three weeks. After the owlets leave the nest, they stay in the same neighborhood as that of their parents. For several months the mother has a strong bond with her babies. She watches them constantly and attacks any animal or person that tries to come near them.

*This vole is no match for a great gray owl. The owl's excellent vision and hearing help it find its prey even when it is hiding in the grass.*

# Great horned owl

If you haven't guessed by now, the mystery owl on page 6 is this magnificent bird, the great horned owl. The word "great" is part of its name because it is one of the largest owls in the world. Perching great horned owls can be as tall as 55 centimeters. It is an awesome sight when this bird spreads its wings in flight. However, when people called this bird "horned," they were really giving it a misleading name. A great horned owl's "horns" are, you guessed it, just feathery ear tufts.

Great horned owls live in just about every place imaginable, from northern evergreen forests to tropical rainforests; from the Arctic to the southern tip of South America. They are comfortable in the mountains as well as in prairies, deserts, and swamps. From time to time you can even spot a great horned owl in a city park.

## "Hooo" is calling?

Great horned owls make the call that we expect all owls to make, which is, "Hoo, hoo-hoo, HOO-HOO!" The hoots carry long distances. Sometimes the owl changes its call from a simple hoot to a chilling scream.

## Early nesters

Great horned owls are among the first birds to nest each year. Sometimes they nest while there is still snow on the ground. The mother-to-be often uses the abandoned nests of other birds or small animals.

## Porcupine for dinner

The great horned owl stalks its prey at dusk and during the night. Because it is larger than most owls, it hunts much bigger animals than others owls do. Its favorite meal is the hare, but this owl also eats skunks, pheasants, fish, and rodents. It has even been known to feast on a porcupine from time to time by turning the animal over and tearing at its soft belly.

# Screech owls

*Eastern screech owls*

There are quite a few types of small owls, so it is often difficult to tell them apart. However, you can always identify a screech owl by the shape of its head. Screech owls are the only small owls that have tufts of feathers. The great horned owl and the long-eared owl also have these tufts, but they are much larger owls.

## Eastern and western screeches

There are around thirty kinds of screech owls throughout the world. Two North American species, the eastern and western screech owls, look similar but also have important differences. Western screech owls are usually around 20 centimeters tall, while their eastern relatives are a centimeter or two smaller. The eastern screech owls live east of the Rocky Mountains; the western screech owls live to the west of the mountain range. The western owls are darker and their calls are different. Eastern screech owls make a long whinnying sound like that of a horse. The call of the western birds begins slowly and gradually speeds up.

## Now you see them, ...

Some screech owls are reddish-brown, while others are gray. In one nest there can be both red and gray screech owls. Owls of both colors roost in trees that match their particular colors.

If you surprise a screech owl, it will freeze bolt upright, suck in its belly, stretch up as tall as it can, and stick its ear tufts up high. By pretending to be a tree trunk, the screech owl blends into its environment and hides from its predators. You have to look really hard to see one of these tricky little owls!

## Where to find them

Screech owls live in mixed evergreen and deciduous woodlands, orchards, and small woodlots. If you want to see a screech owl, look on the ground under a tree for pellets or whitewash. Then look for a woodpecker hole in the tree trunk and watch it carefully. You may soon see a small face appear at the entrance even though this owl usually comes out at night. You can even try this in the city because, unlike many owls, screech owls have adapted to living in cities and towns.

## Extra fat

Only screech owls that live in the mountains migrate in the winter. During the colder months they move into the protected valleys. Screeches that remain in the same habitat all year long handle the harsh weather by conserving their energy. Some of them stop moving altogether during periods of bad weather. When they can't get fresh prey for a day or so, they live off their fat, which is a form of stored energy.

*A western screech owl*

# Flammulated owl

In the dry evergreen woods of the western United States, the beautiful dark-eyed flammulated owl shows off its spectacular colors. Flammulated means "flame." This owl is named for the markings on its feathers that appear like cinnamon, silver-gray, and black-and-white colored flames.

## Hiding out

At only 13 centimeters, this tiny bird is one of the smaller owls in the world, so it must be careful not to be eaten by larger birds and animals. Since it is a type of screech owl, it hides the same way other screech owls do during the daytime. It perches on the branch of a tree whose bark matches the colors of its feathers. In this way, it is camouflaged from its predators.

## A tricky voice

The flammulated owl has an ability that makes it even more difficult to find. It can throw its voice so that the sound it is making seems to be coming from somewhere else. If you look for this little owl in a bush, it is probably in a nearby tree. If you look for it in a tree, well, it might just be in a clump of grass or in a patch of thistles a few feet away. The trick in spotting a flammulated owl is to look where it isn't!

# Whiskered owl

**A** fistful of long, catlike whiskers helps identify the whiskered owl. Sometimes called a spotted screech owl, this small bird has a few blotches of white on its wing feathers. Its whiskers, spots, and distinct call make it different from its screech-owl relatives. Like the other screeches, it is nocturnal. The whiskered owl makes one call that sounds like, "hoo-hoo hooo hoo, hoo-hoo hooo hoo." Its other call is a series of high-pitched "boos" that slow down at the end.

## Dry, hot places

Not much is known about these small, mysterious owls. They are only about 15 centimeters tall when roosting. They live mostly in the mountain canyons of southern Arizona and New Mexico and just north of the Mexican border. They like dry mountain forests and roost in pine, oak, and sycamore trees. Their favorite nesting places are in old holes once drilled by woodpeckers called flickers.

# Spotted owl

Trying to spot a spotted owl is especially difficult. These owls are becoming quite rare. They like living in coniferous forests and these forests are being cut down for paper and lumber products. If you were lucky enough to see a spotted owl, it would be on the west coast near the ocean. Spotted owls make their homes as far north as southwestern British Columbia and as far south as Mexico.

## Close relatives

Spotted owls and barred owls resemble each other. They are both large brown birds with dark eyes. Most other owls have yellow eyes.

# Barred owl

Who cooks for you? Who cooks for you all?" This is what the barred owl seems to be saying when it makes one of its many hooting calls. Perhaps it asks this question because it doesn't have to worry about its own dinner. The barred owl is an excellent hunter and can easily find its prey on the darkest of nights. Its favorite foods are hares, squirrels, and mice. When these are not available, this owl also eats fish, frogs, and birds.

## Friendly owls

The barred owl is found in Canada and across the United States. This large owl can be as tall as 46 centimeters. It isn't shy and often allows people to come quite close to it except during nesting time.

*A barred owl*

*The spotted owl is a large owl. Its perching height is about 41 centimeters.*

31

# Burrowing owl

## Burrow borrowers

The burrowing owl could be called the "borrowing owl," as it does not really burrow its own hole. It borrows holes that have been burrowed by other creatures, such as gophers. Still, it often has to do some burrowing to improve a hole and make it suitable for nesting.

Since this owl doesn't need trees, it can live in prairie regions. In its underground nest the female lays six to ten eggs. Her mate helps her keep the eggs warm for four weeks. Both parents feed the owlets after they hatch.

The burrowing owl has less-developed facial disks because it does not have to rely as much on its hearing as many other owls do. It hunts its favorite meal, the beetle, in the early evening while it is still light outside. For this reason its vision is more important to the burrowing owl than its hearing.

**W**hat a strange name for an owl! Its habit of making its nest in abandoned gopher or badger burrows is stranger yet! A burrowing owl is about 20 centimeters tall while perching and 25 centimeters as shown here. This unusual owl looks as if it is walking on stilts! Its long legs and toes are unfeathered, as such feathers would get constantly dirty when the owl scurries into its burrow. When this bird is alarmed, it hisses or cackles, bends its knees, bobs up and down, and dives into its burrow.

# Boreal owl

The word "boreal" means north. The boreal owl spends most of its summer in the northern forests of Canada, but in winter this owl migrates as far south as the northern United States.

The boreal owl is rarely seen by people. As it hunts at night, it is especially hard to find during the day. Those who are lucky enough to spot one often find the surprised expression on this bird's face quite amusing. Some people claim that this little owl is tame enough to touch!

## A quiet "ting"

The boreal owl is a small owl, around 18 centimeters, that often perches on the lower branches of trees during the day. If you ever hear a "ting, ting, ting," you will either find a faucet dripping or a boreal owl, for that is the sound of its call.

# Snowy owl

The snowy owl looks as if it is bundled up in a white snowsuit! Even its black, hooked talons are almost totally smothered in feathers. Its bright yellow eyes seem to glow. Snowy owls are huge birds, measuring about 50 centimeters from head to toe when they perch. Their full length, as shown here, is closer to 60 centimeters.

## Blending into the white wilderness

Snowy owls are the color of snow for a good reason. They live on the cold arctic tundra where there are no trees. The far north is the usual home of these beautiful birds, but they have been spotted throughout Canada and in the northern United States. From time to time they travel as far south as California, Texas, Missouri, and the Carolinas.

## Living on lemmings

The snowy owl hunts and eats animals that live on the tundra. Its favorite food is the lemming. A lemming looks somewhat like a squirrel with a short tail. (See the picture on page 15.) Lemmings are usually plentiful on the tundra, but every five years or so, their population suddenly drops. During these times the hungry snowy owl must fly south to hunt other animals such as squirrels, mice, rabbits, birds, and fish. It often lands at airports because the big, open fields remind this beautiful bird of the tundra.

## Waiting for lunch to run by

During the arctic summers, the sun shines almost all day long. As a result the snowy owl has adapted to hunting both during the day and night.

As a hunter the snowy owl is big and powerful but not very fast. Instead of going after its prey, the snowy waits for its prey to run by. The snowy perches for a long time without moving, its white feathers making it nearly invisible against the snow. The lemmings that scurry by don't see it until it is too late. The snowy then pounces on its prey, grasping it in its strong talons.

Adult male snowy owls are almost totally white, but the females have dark brown spots on their wings and bands on their tails. Like other owls the females are a little larger than the males. The snowy owl below is guarding her eggs carefully. You can tell she is a female by her pattern. What gender is the snowy owl on the page before?

# Nesting time

Snowy owls build very simple nests on the ground of the arctic tundra. The mother scrapes a round, shallow pit on top of a mound or small hill. She lays from five to eight white or cream-colored eggs. The mother owl sits on the eggs to keep them warm while the father brings her plenty of food.

It takes about a month before the owlets are ready to hatch. At first they are white and fluffy. In a few days they turn a darker color. At this time they look a little like ugly ducklings with their dark-gray downy feathers. It is hard to believe that these owlets will ever have the beautiful white plumage of their parents, but they will! The young birds hatch in the order in which the eggs were laid, so there are owlets of all different ages and colors in the same nest!

## "Playing possum"

The young owlets rely on their parents for food and protection. They cannot fly, but they can swim using their wings as paddles. If they are cornered by a bird or animal, and the situation seems hopeless, they stop moving and "play possum." Since many predators hunt only live prey, the baby owlets hope their acting job is a convincing one.

# Hawk owl

The hawk owl is about 23 centimeters tall when perching. This medium-sized owl is named after the hawk because it looks like a hawk. Both birds have a long, thin tail, which gives them similar profiles. This owl is known for its "frowning" face. Its long, dark eyebrows make it look as if it is unhappy. The eyebrow lines continue so far down the sides of the hawk owl's face that the bird looks as if it has sideburns!

## Mating season is here!

If you hear a hawk owl whistling, you will know that it is mating time. After mating, the hawk owl makes its nest in an open hole, usually in an old tree trunk. The mother lays three to seven eggs in her nest.

Hawk owls hunt by day. In the daylight they can see well, so they rely more on their vision than on their hearing. They make their homes in the central and northern parts of the Canadian Arctic. In these areas the sun shines all night long in the summer!

# Ferruginous pygmy owl

The word "ferruginous" means rust-colored, which is the color of these tiny owls. "Pygmy" means small. At most these owls are only 9 centimeters tall. These tiny birds live in the southern part of the United States, from the Arizona desert to the valleys of the lower Rio Grande River in Texas. Ferruginous owls prefer wooded areas around streams and rivers. Because they like warm climates, they also live in the treed areas of the giant cactus deserts.

## Eyes in the back of its head?

The ferruginous owl looks as if it has eyes in the back of its head. But these "eyes" are really just two black spots outlined in white. Some people think the false eyes are there to fool other birds. When other birds see the eye spots on the back of this owl's head, they think they are looking into the face of a wide-awake owl, even though the owl is probably fast asleep! Although this owl is sometimes active during the day, it is mainly nocturnal.

## Musical owls

Sometime between March and May ferruginous owls choose a nesting hole in a tree or in a giant cactus. They lay three to four eggs. Around nesting time the males sing to their mates for as long as three hours straight. These owls are wonderful singers and can call out from 90 to 150 notes a minute. Their song is so continuous it seems as if the owls never take a breath!

# Northern pygmy owl

"**O**ook," calls the northern pygmy owl, which in owl language might mean, "I've caught a mouse for dinner, so you birds can relax for awhile—but not for long!"

## Mountains and deserts

The northern pygmy owl likes living in mountainous pine forests but can also live in deciduous forests and in dry, hot regions.

If you were a small bird living in a nearby tree, you would not want this whiskered wonder as your neighbor. To a mouse or bird, it is as dangerous as a cat. This quick little owl can even catch insects while flying. Even though a pygmy owl is only 10 centimeters tall, it has a huge appetite. It hunts day and night, but mostly at night. As tiny as this owl is, it can kill a bird or animal much bigger than itself.

## Get lost!

One trick that other birds use to make this owl leave their territory is the scare tactic. They get together in groups, flap their wings like mad, and try to scare the little owl away. They tweet and screech in their scariest voices and make an unearthly racket. If that doesn't work, they had better hope that there are plenty of mice around so the pygmy owl will leave them alone!

*The ferruginous and northern pygmy owls are the only owls with black streaks along their sides. Their long tails are barred with white. When these owls perch, their tails stick out past their wings. Both birds have protective eye spots on the backs of their heads.*

# Elf owl

This round little bird is so small it could fit into a teacup! At just 8 centimeters tall, the elf owl is the smallest owl in the world! Instead of having a large head for its body as other owls do, the elf owl is small all over. It has a short tail and no ear tufts, but it does have quite large feet.

## A spiny home

Elf owls sometimes make their homes in tree holes, but their favorite nesting places are in the giant cacti that are found in Mexico and in the southwestern American desert regions. The tiny owls make their nests in the holes carved by other birds such as flickers.

Why might the elf owl make its home in a giant cactus? This tiny bird needs the prickly needles of the cactus to protect it from its predators. If a predator was able to get past the cactus spines and catch this bird, the elf owl would likely "play possum" until it was left alone.

## Small owl, big food

During the daytime elf owls stay inside their holes or hide among thick leaves. In the evening they come out to hunt their favorite meal—big juicy bugs. Sometimes they enjoy a change in their diets and eat a small mouse instead. A mouse is a big meal for the tiny elf owl!

## A yelling elf

The elf owl's call is very loud for such a small bird. Its yell sounds something like a cackle and can scare away even large animals. This tiny owl also makes a less frightening call that sounds like "choo-choo-choo-choo." Perhaps it wishes it could take a train trip!

*Both the pygmy owls and the elf owl like living in hot places. One of these hot places is Arizona, where these giant cacti grow. They make good homes for tiny owls because the sharp needles protect them from predators.*

# Saw-whet owl

Some people claim that saw-whet owls are so tame that you can touch them. If you were able to pick up this owl, you could hold it in the palm of your hand! It is only 15 centimeters tall!

## Scratchy voices

The saw-whet gets its unusual name from the sound of its voice. The word "whet" means to sharpen. Some people think that this little owl's cry sounds like the noise a saw makes when it is being sharpened. Fortunately for the people or animals that are nearby, this scratchy cry is not used very often. The saw-whet's most common call is a soothing, short, ringing note that sounds like a bell from far away.

## Cozy home

The saw-whet lives in Alaska, Canada, and as far south as the central part of the United States. Like other small owls, it often chooses a woodpecker hole for its nest. Inside the hole the little owl lines the walls with soft mosses, leaves, bits of bark, and twigs. When the owlets hatch, they nestle together in their cozy, safe home.

## Seven hungry babies

The saw-whet can have as many as seven hungry owlets to feed. Both mother and father combine their hunting skills to bring home enough food for their family. At night they hunt their favorite food—mice. Saw-whets also eat squirrels, bats, birds, and insects.

*This baby saw-whet has downy feathers. Notice how soft the outer edges of its facial disks seem compared to the fully developed disks of its mother.*

# Nesting

*A male snowy owl courting a female snowy*

**D**uring the winter a male owl makes loud and frequent calls into the cold night air. He wants to make sure that other male owls will stay out of his territory now that it is time for him to attract a mate. In order to do this, he makes flying tours above his area, constantly on the lookout for a possible mate. If all goes well, he will find a female owl in late winter.

## Owl has gone a-courting

Once the couple meets, it takes a while for them to get acquainted. The male owl tries to show the female that he will be a good provider for their owlets. He may perform trick flights and present her with mice or lemmings.

## Getting a nest ready

The female owl looks for a nesting spot long before it is time to lay her eggs. Since owls do not make their own nests, they either adopt the abandoned nest of another bird or use a natural nesting area. Their favorite nesting place is often a hole in a tree or the crook of two joining branches. Other owls lay their eggs on the rocky ledges of cliffs or in shallow holes on the ground.

Even though the female does not make the nest, she takes great care choosing just the right spot for her family. In the nest she spends a lot of time scratching the floor and rearranging the twigs. The male owl rarely enters the nest but often watches his mate as she does all the work!

## The incubation period

A female owl lays between three and twelve eggs. If there is a lot of food that year, she may have two broods of owlets. All owl eggs are white or cream colored and vary from round to oval. A female owl lays an egg every few days rather than one after the other. The eggs hatch a few days apart so each owlet receives the care it needs when it is first hatched.

The new mother keeps her eggs under her stomach where she has plucked out some feathers. This bare spot allows her body heat to pass through to the eggs. From time to time she turns the eggs over with her feet and beak so that each side receives an even amount of warmth. She wets her feathers because it is important for the eggs to stay moist as they are developing. The time spent waiting for the eggs to hatch is called the **incubation period**.

During this time the mother owl cannot leave the nest because her eggs would get too cold and the unhatched chicks would die. The male owl brings food to her while she keeps the eggs warm.

*A short-eared owl makes her nest on the ground.*

## An owlet hatches

After one month, an owlet is ready to break open its egg. It uses its egg tooth to crack the shell. This tooth is on the upper part of its beak and falls off about ten days after the owlet has hatched.

The owlet emerges blind and wet. It cannot hold up its head because its neck is too weak. As it dries off, it fluffs up its soft coat of down. At one week of age the baby owl is quite an ugly sight as its soft down is being replaced by bristly feathers. Its wing feathers grow in a little later.

## Bring us more food!

About a day after hatching the mother owl starts feeding her young. She takes an insect or a piece of prey and offers it to the owlet. The food is coated with the mother's saliva, so it goes down the owlet's throat easily. An owlet is very demanding. It eats more when it is young than when it is an adult because it needs a lot of food in order to grow. Together, the mother owl and the owlets cry out constantly to the father for more food. As the weather gets warmer and the owlets want even more to eat, the mother owl joins the father in the endless search for more food. Within a few weeks the owlets have doubled in size.

## What is imprinting?

Owls have a great habit of cocking their heads to the side when they are looking at something. As an owlet begins to see, it turns its head from side to side in order to focus on its surroundings. Since the owlet seems to be moving its head in the shape of a triangle, this movement is called **triangulation**. Triangulation begins approximately twelve days after an owlet has hatched. It is a very important stage in its development because, at the same time as it is learning to see, the tiny bird is also learning who its parents are and to what species it belongs.

*Five-day-old great horned owlets in their nest*

The living creatures that an owl sees most often during its first days of life are what it considers to be its parents. After twenty-one days it is fully able to recognize them. When a baby owlet recognizes its parents, it has **imprinted** on them. That means that the appearance of the parents is fixed in the owlet's memory. Later on, when the grown owl is looking for a mate, it will look for an owl that has the same body shape and makes the same sounds as its parents do.

## "Who are you?"

Sometimes people find a baby owl and take it home, thinking that they are saving its life. In most cases the parents of the owlet have not abandoned it but are simply searching for food. If an owlet is taken away from its parents when it is beginning to triangulate, it imprints on the person who takes care of it. Soon it will only relate to human beings and will be afraid of other owls. You can see how important it is that an owlet remain with its parents. Otherwise it will never know who it really is.

Even if such an owl was set free, it would still look for someone with the same shape of head and the same hair as the person it first saw. When an owl that has imprinted on a human being tries to find a mate, it will follow a person with a familiar appearance. Unfortunately, most owls that follow people around are shot because the people they are following don't understand why the birds are acting so strangely.

# Owl conservation

Owls may be beautiful and fascinating creatures, but not many of us ever see them. They live in the wilderness far away from human eyes. But this is not the only reason they are hard to find. There are fewer and fewer owls in the world each year.

Why are there fewer owls than there used to be? One reason is that people have destroyed the places where owls live. When forests are cut down, many owls lose their homes. When prairie fields are ploughed and wetlands drained, even more owl homes disappear. As we continue to develop the earth's wilderness, there is less room left for other living creatures.

## Toxic chemicals

Many creatures, including owls, die because there are **toxins** in their food. Toxins are harmful chemicals. Industries and farms use large amounts of these dangerous chemical toxins. Chemicals released onto the earth eventually end up in our water and food. When living creatures eat polluted food and water, the toxins build up in their bodies. Owls, like other living things, can become sick and even die from toxins.

## Uncaring humans

Many owls are injured or lose their lives each year because they are hit by cars or trucks. Owls flying at night are blinded by oncoming traffic and are then hit.

Owls are also injured and killed by people with shotguns. Some people believe that owls are dangerous creatures because they are predators. They think that owls are a threat to them and, without thinking, they shoot.

## Killing with kindness

What would you do if you found a baby owl outside its nest? You might think that you could help the owlet by looking after it. Unfortunately, too many people pick up owls and take them home without knowing how to feed or care for them. Wild birds that aren't properly taken care of suffer and could die.

## Finding an owl

If you happen to find an injured or baby owl that seems to be all alone, do not touch it. Go as far away as you can from it but still keep it in sight. Stay quiet and watch for at least half an hour. If the bird is still by itself after this length of time, phone your local animal shelter.

*The burrowing owl is in trouble.*

*The barn owl is threatened in many North American areas.*

Someone there will be able to help you or can tell you where to find the nearest bird **rehabilitation center**. Some countries have special owl rehabilitation centers that look after injuries, teach owls to hunt, and give them a place to live before returning them to the wild.

## Owls in trouble

Owls face many dangers, and several species have not been able to cope. Some owls are **threatened**, some are **endangered**, and some are **rare**. The barn owl is an example of a threatened bird. It is on its way to becoming endangered in some places. The great gray owl, the flammulated owl, the hawk owl, and the spotted owl are also in trouble in many areas of North America. Endangered animals often become extinct before people even realize they are rare. When an owl becomes extinct, that owl has disappeared from the earth forever. What a sad thought!

*A cage at Kay McKeever's home for owls*

*This short-eared owl imprinted on people and now lives right in Kay's house.*

# Giving a hoot about owls

If you are interested in conservation and want to learn how to protect owls, the first thing you should do is learn all about these wonderful birds. When you know about their habitats and their basic needs, you will be able to teach other people about owls, too. Once people understand owls, they will be much more interested in keeping them around. Conserving owls and all wildlife is something in which everyone can take part. Help owls! Give a hoot!

## There is hope!

With all the terrible tales of people hurting or killing owls, it is easy to lose hope. Fortunately, there are caring people who are interested in saving these birds. Important work is being carried out by biologists who study owls in their natural environments. There are researchers doing valuable laboratory studies on owls all over the world. People also operate owl breeding stations where much is being learned about owl relationships.

# Kay McKeever's home for owls

Kay McKeever is an example of a person making a difference in the lives of owls. Kay has been rescuing, nursing, and releasing owls for many years. She is the founder and director of the Owl Research and Rehabilitation Foundation in Vineland, Ontario. She is known all over the world for her work with owls.

Kay and her husband Larry care for over one hundred owls. They keep the owls in outdoor cages specially designed to allow the birds to fly around. Many of the cages are huge and come equipped with trees, perches, pools, and platforms.

People from all over the continent arrive on Kay's doorstep with injured owls and owlets. Some of the owls are so badly hurt that they die. Others can be rehabilitated and returned to the wild. There are still others that get better but, because of a damaged eye or broken wing, will never be able to go free. Many of the owls that stay on at Kay and Larry's end up having owlets that are later released into the wild. Several act as foster parents to other orphaned owls.

Running the station at Vineland is a full-time job for Kay and Larry. Imagine having to feed 250 mice a day to over one hundred owls, maintaining more than fifty large cages, and caring for each individual owl and its particular problem! Kay also spends a great deal of time writing, giving talks, being interviewed, and teaching people about owls. Many different people help Kay by sending her donations to assist in the running of her facility. Because of people such as Kay McKeever, there is hope for wildlife—especially owls!

*Kay McKeever with Granny, a spectacled owl, one of Kay's oldest foster-parent owls*

# Glen Loates

**E**ver since Glen Loates was a child, his love of animals has led him to try capturing our natural world in drawings, paintings, and sculpture. As a boy he spent as much time as he could exploring neighborhood streams and woods. He started sketching interesting scenes during hikes and used these sketches to do more detailed illustrations.

Now, as a professional artist, Glen works in a light-filled studio in his own home. He has a natural history library and often borrows materials, such as animal pelts, from museums to help him make his paintings as realistic as possible. Glen also uses wildlife video tapes, clippings, and photographs from nature magazines as reference material for his work. Yet, no matter how much time Glen spends in the studio, he still thinks of the wilderness as his real working space.

## A word from Glen

When I was a young boy just learning to draw, I was frustrated because I could not make my pictures realistic enough. Before long, though, I found out that I could greatly improve my sketches by doing them over and over. I took time to sketch every single day and, as if by by magic, my hands began to draw what my eyes were seeing.

If you are a budding nature artist, the best thing you can do is to draw as much as possible. Keep a daily sketchbook and hold onto both your good and bad drawings because they will help you see just how much your work has improved. If you start a collection of photographs and magazine clippings, you will have plenty of reference material to help you with your practise sketching—but don't just work with other people's pictures. Take as many field trips as possible and create your own impressions of nature.

## Sketching the saw-whet owl

The saw-whet owl is one of Glen's favorite subjects because it reminds him of a Persian cat. On one of Glen's field trips he discovered some owl pellets at the base of a tree. He tapped the bottom of the trunk with a stick, and soon a saw-whet owl popped its catlike face out of the hole in the tree. The saw-whet was just as curious to see Glen as Glen was to see the owl.

After Glen has made a series of field sketches, he often makes more detailed pencil drawings of his subjects, such as these pictures of the saw-whet owl. He then does finished paintings or sculptures of certain animals.

Saw-whet Owl

55

# Glossary

**abandoned** - Given up and left alone.

**adapted** - Having made changes to fit new situations or surroundings.

**anatomy** - The structure of an animal or plant.

**barred** - Covered in stripe-like markings.

**brood** - The young birds that hatch from a single set of eggs.

**camouflage** - To change the look or actions of something in order to disguise it.

**cell** - The smallest basic unit in a living being. When cells are joined together in a certain way they become animals and plants.

**coniferous** (tree) - A tree that has cones.

**conservation** - Protecting our natural resources from harm.

**deciduous** (tree) - A tree that loses its leaves.

**endangered** - Very close to no longer existing.

**environment** - The surroundings in which an animal or plant lives.

**extinct** - No longer living or existing.

**identification** - A unique feature that helps prove what something is.

**indigestible** - Something that cannot be broken down and digested in the stomach.

**lemming** - A squirrel-like arctic rodent with a small tail.

**mating** - The joining together of two animals of one species to produce offspring.

**migrate** - To move from one area to another during certain seasons. Many birds migrate south for the winter.

**molting** - The process of old feathers, skin, or hair falling out and being replaced by new growth.

**owlet** - A young owl.

**pelt** - The skin of an animal including its fur or hair.

**"playing possum"** - Pretending to be ill or dead.

**plumage** - The feathers which cover a bird.

**population** - The total number of people or animals living in an area.

**predator** - An animal, such as a hawk or wolf, that eats other animals.

**prey** - An animal that is hunted and eaten by another animal.

**rare** - In very low numbers or living in very few places.

**rehabilitation** - Restoring something to a healthy state.

**rodent** - A mammal that has large front teeth used for gnawing. Mice, voles, and squirrels are all examples of rodents.

**roost** - The place where a bird rests.

**species** - A distinct animal or plant group that shares similar charactersitics and can produce offspring within its group.

**supernatural** - Something that lives outside the ordinary, natural world. Ghosts and spirits are said to be supernatural.

**superstition** - A belief based on fear of the unknown. The idea that a black cat crossing your path brings bad luck is a supersition.

**sycamore** - A North American tree whose bark often flakes off in large pieces and whose leaves look like maple leaves.

**threatened** - Needing protection from becoming extinct.

**tropical** - The areas on either side of the equator that have the warmest temperatures on earth.

**tundra** - The most northern regions of North America, Asia, and Europe where no trees grow. The ground beneath the tundra is always frozen.

# Index

3456789 BP Printed in Canada 7654321098